Beautiful
and Her Mini-Me?!

A BOXER DOG STORY

Marion Harley
Author, Illustrator, and Photographer

Beautiful Bella and Her Mini-Me?!
A Boxer Dog Story

Copyright 2023 by Marion Harley
(Registration TXu 2-316-951, United States Copyright Office)

Written, Illustrated and Photographed by Marion Harley

Courier Publishing
Greenville, South Carolina

PRINTED IN THE UNITED STATES OF AMERICA

All rights reserved.

ISBN: 978-1-955295-28-4

Library of Congress Control Number: 2023905311

Dedication

This book is dedicated to my Heavenly Father, for GOD, You are the Giver of Life (Psalm 36:9).

O Lord, Giver of Life, You are Bread for the world! You open our eyes to light!!

Acknowledgments

Complete thanks to my husband, Paul Orville Harley, and to my daughter, Savienne Michelle Mitchell, for helping to create great memories by appearing in photos and lending their ongoing support in bringing to life my story about Bella and her pup.

I also wish to acknowledge Butch Blume and the Courier Publishing team. Thank you for your great advice and longstanding support.

Dear Reader,

    The Boxer breed was first imported to the United States after World War I. Boxers became popular in the late 1930s and are now the fourteenth most popular breed in the country. They are also the number three "Most Loyal Dog."

    The breed has won "Best in Show" at The Westminster Kennel Club Dog Show four times: in 1947, 1949, 1951, and 1970.

    The typical Boxer is intelligent, highly alert, and fearless. Yet Boxers are friendly and playful dogs who like to stay busy.

    They can become bored with repetition. In spite of its heritage as a powerful and courageous hunter, a Boxer is happiest when he is with his family, especially children. He is protective and patient with kids and makes an ideal family dog. Boxers will fiercely guard their family and home against strangers.

    Boxers have earned their name because they try to show affection by pawing at you, not unlike a human boxer sparring in a ring. They will stand on their back legs and paw at you in an attempt to play with you or gain your attention.

    Here's hoping you enjoy this informative read about the birth of a Boxer pup and his first nine weeks of life. Happy reading!

Marion Harley

It was Thursday, July 29, 2021, early in the morn.
It was obvious that a wee little one was about to be born.
It was a welcomed event because Beautiful Bella was over
      eight years old, you see,
Thought by most that she would never become a
      mother-to-be.

So, we worked diligently all morning to prepare
Bella's whelping box, using great care.

We had just added the last strip of tape
When we glanced to our right and saw a miniature shape.

Bella had given birth without making a sound.
She had removed the thin sac and there lay her puppy,
cute and round.

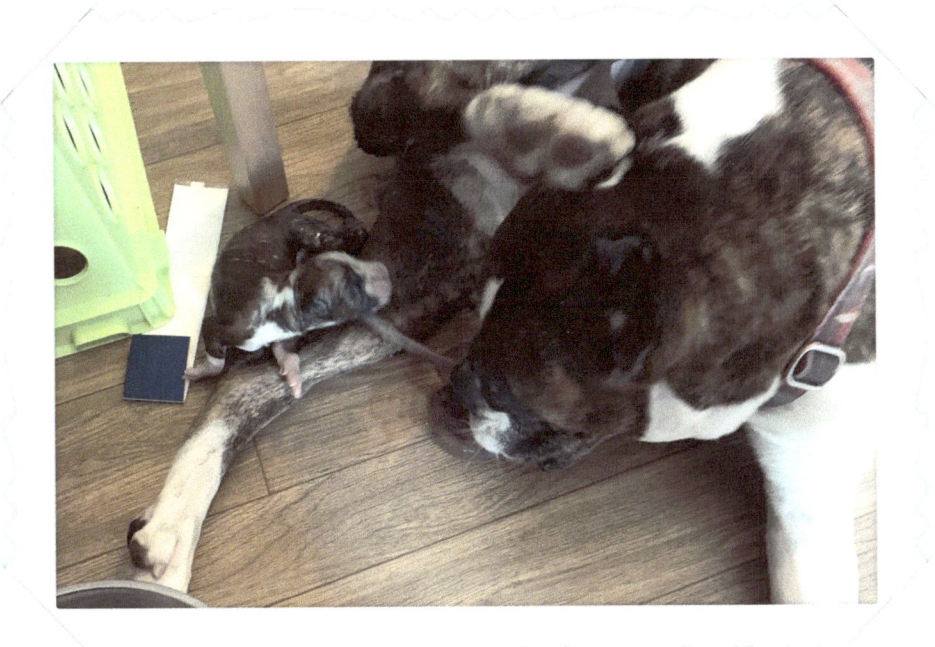

Bella licked her new pup until he was sparkling clean.
She kept him warm, and puppy nursing was often seen.

He had a black coating over his brown fur,
Which made us assume he would have black stripes,
    just like her.

We bundled up mother and child for baby's first car ride.
We were off to visit the vet, whose advice we will
use as a valuable guide.

On day two, Baby Bella tired of his mother fussing over him — he'd had quite enough!
So we heard our two-day-old puppy growl at his mother, and it sounded rather gruff!!

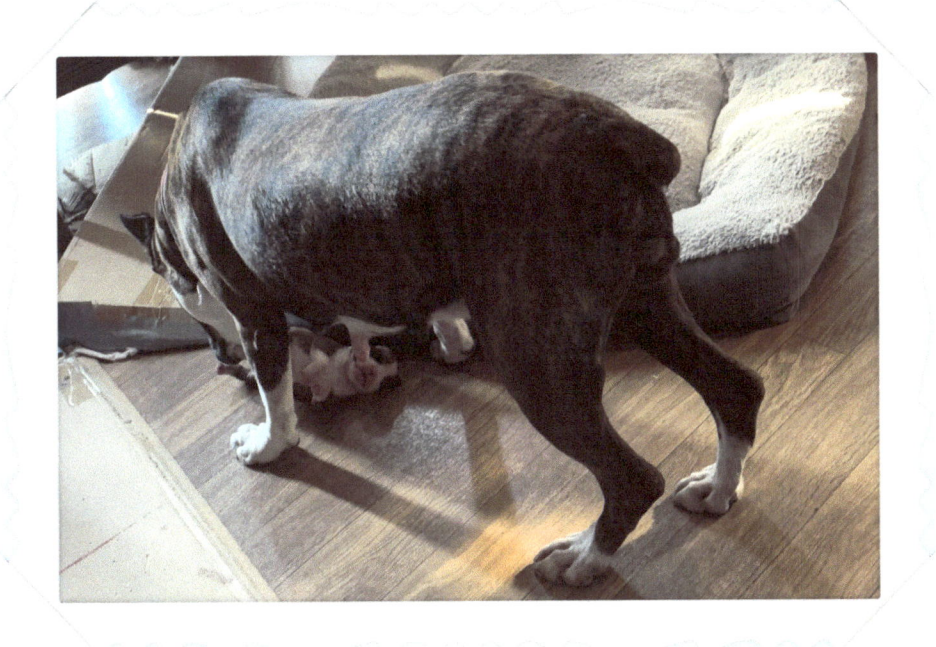

On day three, Puppy had his second visit to the vet to have his tail docked and his dewclaws removed.
Both procedures were done for maintaining good health and for defining and preserving the Boxer breed character which AKC had unequivocally approved.

In week one, Baby Bella's eyes stayed closed,
But he was able to navigate around by smelling with his nose.
He could not hear or see.
Staying close to Mom is where he wanted to be.

During week two, Mother Bella carried her "mini-me'
 around a lot.
She kept him very close to her heart.
Bella made sure the two of them were always touching
 and near.
She wanted her little one to have NO fear.

By the end of week two, it was decided his name
    should be DUKE.
We knew he could hear when loud noises left him spooked.
He crawled around on his belly searching for
    a lunch meeting,
For mostly life, at this time, was all about
    sleeping and eating.

Week three: Duke has begun to walk and have fun.
We even once caught him managing to run.
A visit to the vet at three weeks old,
Duke had gained a pound a week — so cuddly to hold.

Mom Bella decided, "My son shall have a toy!"
A green dinosaur is what she chose for her boy.
Duke watched it, crawled on it, chewed it,
    and slept with it.
A pup and his dinosaur IS a perfect fit.

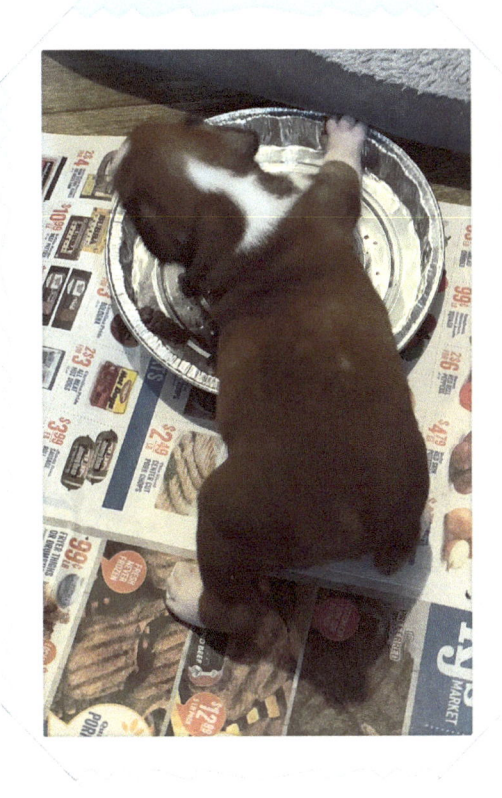

By week four, Duke was eating wet puppy food and drinking water from pie plates.

He loved to play with Mom, toys, and Rory, a four-month old Ruby Cavalier King Charles Spaniel — Duke's new playmate.

He loved to socialize until he was all tuckered out. Then, it became nap time so he could reenergize for his next adventure — no doubt.

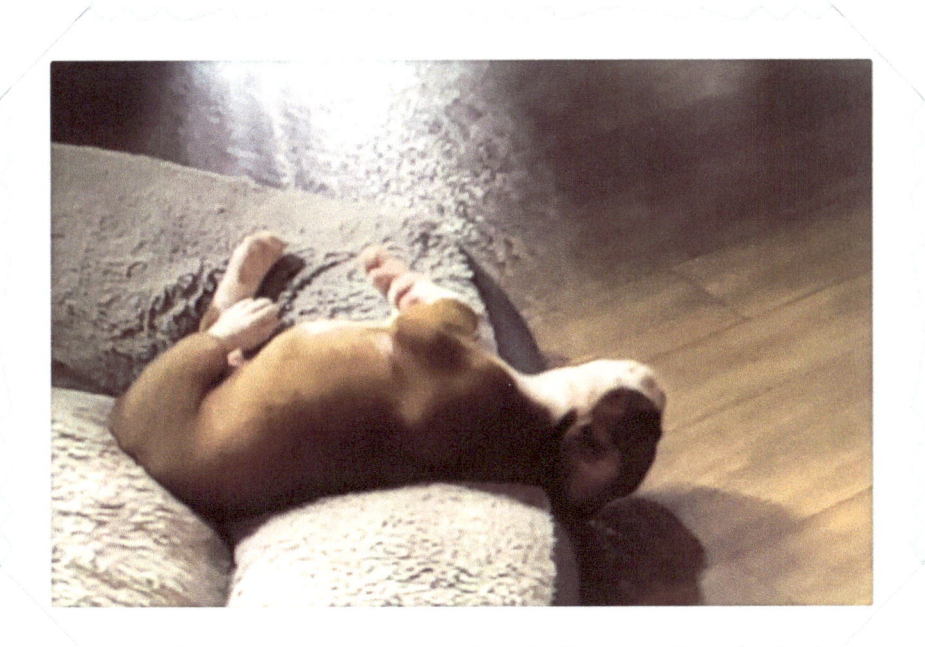

The fifth week of life, Duke loved, loved, loved to sleep in the crevice of his bed.

Look at how much he has grown, from his nub to his head!

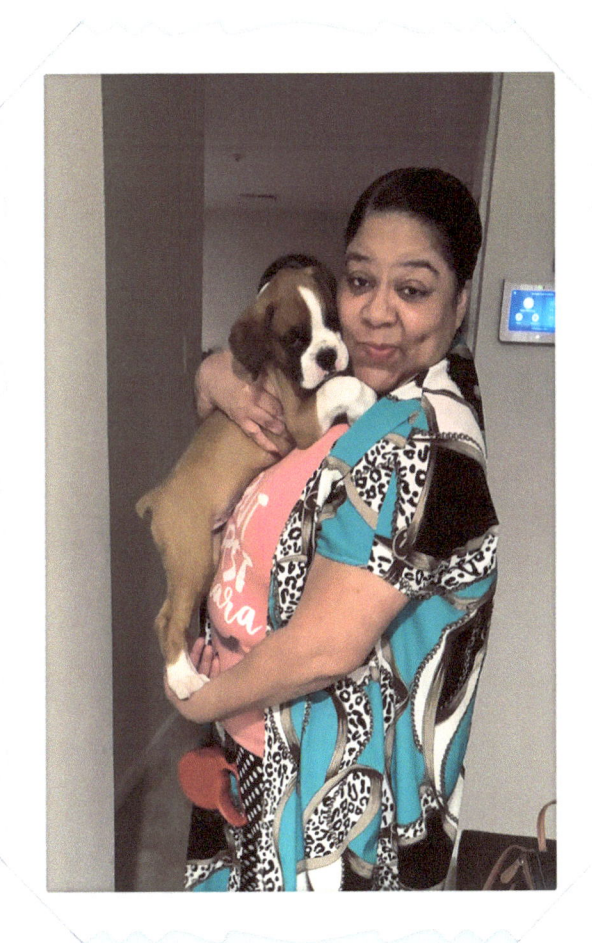

During week six, father met son.
We discovered Duke was not his brindle-mother's
    mini-me, for he had NO stripes like she.
But, he was his father's EXACT lookalike —
    a MINI-HIM!
His dad, Explosive Thunder, is a flashy fawn who has a
    sleek, tan coat, and he is sculptured and trim.

Also, during the sixth week, Duke received a collar to prepare him for outdoor leash walks.
He loved to feel the warmth of the sun and the soft touch of the grass so much that when it was time to go indoors, for a moment he would balk.

During week seven, Mama Bella educated Duke on all necessary skills.
The normal routines of grooming, feeding, exercise, and play time were Duke's ultimate thrills.

Training begins in week eight for this extremely
  intelligent dog.
"Down!" may be the first command to teach, for he jumps
  up and down and leaps about when excited — sort of
  like a frog.

He still takes quite a few naps during the day,
But, given his zeal for adventure, he's always ready to play.

Week nine: Duke has a chiseled, muscular body and is always eager to roam.

Duke took a long vehicle ride from South Carolina to Maryland to meet his new family and see his new home.

At seven months old and settled into his new home,
Duke doesn't want for ANYTHING.
Surrounded by pillows on his new master's bed,
It becomes obvious: Duke is now KING!

CPSIA information can be obtained
at www.ICGtesting.com
Printed in the USA
JSHW072222180423
40475JS00002B/27